Viewpoints

Intermediate
Differentiated Curriculum

Grade Levels	Length of Time
4th – 6th	40+ hours

ISBN   978-1-59363-290-8

Prufrock Press' Differentiated Curriculum Kits provide hands-on, discovery-based, research-oriented activities that are cross-curricular. Prufrock curriculum guides save valuable time, are easy to use, and are highly effective. Each unit begins with a pre-assessment and ends with a post-assessment, so growth and progress can be tracked. Lessons are tied to National and Texas State Standards, freeing teachers to spend more time with students. Each activity is a complete lesson with a focus, closure, extension(s), and suggested assessment opportunities. Differentiated strategies are also identified in every lesson. The evaluation tools are authentic, requiring students to demonstrate knowledge by practical application. Rubrics are provided to help with assessment.

We recognize that one activity cannot reach every student at every ability level, so suggestions are given for modifications. Please feel free to modify activities as needed.

Prufrock curricula are based on conceptual themes. By using abstract words such as *wonders, changes, structures*, and *powers*, the topics are broad, universal, and timeless. Research proves that conceptual learning helps bridge the disciplines requiring higher-order thinking, which in turn leads to meaningful understanding.

Come explore the world of Viewpoints...

Students examine the concept of *viewpoints* from many angles in this program. From the history of child labor laws to optical illusions, *Viewpoints* takes students through a variety of critical thinking activities. Students learn to consider others' perspectives as they learn the process of formal debate. Students re-evaluate their value systems as they are challenged to consider topics such as rich vs. poor, animal rights, and hypothetical situations involving difficult decisions. Students will gain a new understanding of the phrase "walk in another's shoes."

Acknowledgements

We would like to credit Sandra N. Kaplan, Javits Projects, University of Southern California, for the use of the Depth and Complexity Dimensions in our materials.

A special thank you to Suzy Hagar, Executive Director for Advanced Academic Services in the Carrollton-Farmers Branch Independent School District, for project development advice, suggestions, and support.

Written by: Debbie Keiser, Chuck Nusinov, and Mary Hennenfent
Edited by: Debbie Keiser, Brenda McGee, and Linda Triska
Cover Art by: Brandon Bolt
Illustrations: Angie Harrelson

NOTE

The Web sites in this curriculum were working and age-appropriate at the time of publication, but Prufrock Press Inc. has no control over any subsequent changes.

Table of Contents

Checklists   **Page**

Notes

_____

_____

_____

_____

_____

_____

_____

_____

_____

_____

_____

_____

_____

_____

_____

_____

_____

_____

Unit Planner

Concept: Viewpoints
Grade level: 4 - 6
Length of Time: 40+ hours

Diversity

- Racism/politics
- Child labor, housing, war
- Stages of life
- Tolerance for ambiguity
- Rich vs. poor
- Inference

Animals

- Compound eyes
- Development of infants
- *Black Beauty*

Viewpoints

Math

- Statistics
- Graphs
- Math magic
- Logic problems

Communication Arts

- Idioms
- Poetry

Visual

- Optical illusions

Unit Overview

Students examine the concept of viewpoints in this 2003 NAGC Curriculum Award winning differentiated curriculum. From the history of child labor laws to optical illusions, *Viewpoints* takes students through a variety of critical thinking activities. Students learn to consider others' perspectives as they learn the process of formal debate. Students re-evaluate their value systems as they are challenged to consider topics such as rich versus poor, animal rights, and hypothetical situations involving difficult decisions.

Viewpoints are rarely stagnant.

Society's viewpoints may change over time.

Personal viewpoints may be influenced by a person's culture and/or background.

Viewpoints may be manipulated by outside influences.

Guiding Questions for *Viewpoints*

Guiding questions are the factual (F), conceptual (C), and philosophical (P) questions addressed in the curriculum. These are the questions students should be able to answer after completing the activities in this curriculum.

(F) What is a viewpoint?
(F) What is Ginger's perspective on life?
(F) What is mediation?
(F) What is trend extrapolation?
(F) What are compound eyes?
(F) What types of animals have compound eyes?
(F) What is a photographic memory?
(F) What is an inference?
(F) What is a debate?
(F) What are statistics?
(F) What does it mean to be "rich"?
(F) What is an illusion?
(F) What is an idiom?
(F) What is a paradox?

> F= factual question
> C= conceptual question
> P= philosophical question

(C) How would the world change if everyone had the same viewpoint?
(C) How does Black Beauty's viewpoint change during his different jobs?
(C) How does a mediator help people with opposing viewpoints come to an agreement?
(C) Why were child labor laws created by the government?
(C) How did people's perspectives changed concerning child labor from the early 1800's to the early 1900s?
(C) How would compound eyes make your life more difficult?
(C) How does age change your viewpoint?
(C) How are debates and viewpoints related?
(C) How can data in graphs be misleading?
(C) How is the development of animals related to their chance of surviving infancy?
(C) How can idioms be confusing?
(C) How are tricks, math, and magic related?
(C) How can viewpoints be expressed in poetry?
(C) How can viewpoints be expressed in art?
(C) Can only viewing a portion of an object or understanding a portion of a concept skew your point of view?

(P) Should animals be held in captivity?

Notes

_____

_____

_____

_____

_____

_____

_____

_____

_____

_____

_____

_____

_____

_____

_____

_____

_____

_____

_____

_____

_____

_____

_____

Activity 1 – Pre-Assessment

Differentiation Strategies
Multiple Perspectives
- Brainstorming
- Point of View

Ethics/Unanswered Questions
- Provocative Questions
- Problem Finding

Instructional Materials
- chart paper

A. Draw the following picture on the chalkboard.

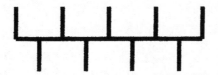

B. Ask students to brainstorm about what the picture could be. Encourage each student to generate at least 20 ideas in 5 minutes.

C. Have students share their lists with the class. Ask that they listen and mark off any ideas shared by other students. They should share only new ideas. Record all responses on a large piece of chart paper.

D. Ask the following questions: What do you think a football coach would say about the drawing? (It looks like four goalposts side by side.) What do you think a builder would say about the drawing? (It looks like two layers of brick on a house.)

E. Tell students these are **viewpoints**. Ask for a general definition of viewpoints and write it at the bottom of the chart paper.

F. Keep the chart paper for use at the end of the unit.

Activity 2 - Diverse Viewpoints

Differentiation Strategies

Knowledge and Skills
- Attributes
- Categorization

Analysis and Synthesis
- Convergent and Divergent Thinking
- Creative Problem Solving

Ethics/Unanswered Questions
- Provocative Questions
- Aesthetic Thinking

Multiple Perspectives
- Brainstorming
- Group Consensus

Instructional Materials
- Drawing materials

> ### Enduring Understanding
> Viewpoints are rarely stagnant.
>
> ### Guiding Questions
> (F) What is a viewpoint?
> (C) How would the world change if everyone had the same viewpoint?

A. Ask the following questions: What if everyone in the world had the same viewpoint on every subject? What if everyone thought alike?

B. Encourage students to look at these questions from many viewpoints. Ask the following guiding questions: How would **politics** change? How would **racism** change? How would wars change? How would history be changed?

C. Have students form several groups. Have each group choose a question or point discussed during the previous step. Ask each group to brainstorm all the things that would change about the subject if everyone had the same point of view.

D. Ask each team to compile its brainstormed ideas into an essay. The essays should include at least eight ways the topic would be different. The students should also evaluate whether everyone having the same point of view on the topic would be better for the world.

> ### Teacher Tip
> Rubrics are an effective assessment tool in evaluating student performance in areas which are complex and vague. By allowing students to see what the expectations are before they begin the assignment, work quality improves dramatically.

E. Have students create a **graphic organizer** to represent their essays and review the Evaluation Rubric on Attachment 1 by which this assignment will be assessed.

Closure
Ask students to share their essays and graphic organizers.

Extensions
A. Pose the following question for discussion: Are there any viewpoints that never change?

B. For a math extension, ask students how people view math in different ways. What personality types enjoy math? What types dislike math? Have students discuss why there are so many different viewpoints about school subjects.

Assessment
Evaluate graphic organizers and essays using the rubric on Attachment 1.

Notes

_____

_____

_____

_____

_____

_____

_____

_____

_____

_____

_____

_____

Activity 3 – Animal Viewpoints

Differentiation Strategies
Knowledge and Skills
- Inferences
- Attributes

Analysis and Synthesis
- Analogies
- Aesthetic Thinking

Multiple Perspectives
- Shared Inquiry
- Point of View

Enduring Understanding
Society's viewpoints may change over time.

Guiding Questions
(F) What is Ginger's perspective on life?
(F) What is an inference?
(C) How does Black Beauty's viewpoint change during his different jobs?

Instructional Materials
- multiple matching copies of *Black Beauty* book, by Anna Sewell
- computer with Internet access

Note
The Web sites in this curriculum were working and age-appropriate at the time of publication, but Prufrock Press Inc. has no control over any subsequent changes. Please preview all sites before letting students view them.

A. Locate multiple copies of *Black Beauty*. Be sure you find matching copies. (They can be abridged or unabridged.) One version can be read on the below Web site.
http://literatureproject.com/book/sewell/black-beauty/index.htm

Another option to is to purchase the book on audiotape and allow students to listen to it.

B. Read or listen to *Black Beauty* with students. You may wish to complete this activity over several weeks.

C. As you read each chapter, discuss Black Beauty's point of view during his different jobs. Discuss Ginger's **perspective** on life. Discuss Black Beauty's mother's perspective on life.

Closure

After reading the book, have students complete the Six Hat Thinking assignment on Attachment 2. Have students work with you to create a rubric (use the blank rubric on Attachment 3) or use Attachment 1 to guide in the evaluation of this project.

Extensions

A. Have students write a book review for their favorite online book store that offers this opportunity.

Teacher Tip
Six Thinking Hats
created by Dr. de Bono in the 1980s.
White Hat – Facts
Red Hat – Feeling and emotions
Black Hat – Judgment and caution
Yellow Hat – Logical and Positive
Green Hat – Creativity
Blue Hat – Process Control

B. Have students view the *Black Beauty* movie and compare and contrast the differences between the book and movie.

C. Ask students to find other books written from unusual perspectives and share them with the class.

D. Have students explore the concept of **horse whispering** made popular by a book and movie. Visit the following Web site:
http://www.equine-behavior.com/origins_of_horse_whispering.htm

E. Encourage students to further their research on horses by exploring the following mathematical questions:
- How much does a horse eat in one year? How does this compare to a human?
- How many horses can be pastured on a given acreage?
- Are there different top speeds for horses on different terrains? What are the differences?

Assessment

Evaluate the Closure activity using the rubric created by the students or the rubric on Attachment 1.

Notes

_____

_____

_____

_____

_____

Activity 4 – Apartments vs. Condos

Differentiation Strategies
Analysis and Synthesis
- Problem Defining
- Evaluate Situations

Multiple Perspectives
- Debate
- Brainstorming

Relevance and Significance
- Role Playing
- Simulation

Enduring Understanding
Personal viewpoints may be influenced by a person's culture and/or background.

Guiding Questions
(F) What is mediation?
(C) How does a mediator help people with opposing viewpoints come to an agreement?

A. Explain that a **hypothetical** situation is a fictional event that could take place. Pose the following hypothetical situation:

A **landlord** has agreed to sell a **dilapidated** apartment complex to the city of Dallas, Texas. The city plans to tear down the complex and build 100 condominiums in its place. The current **tenants** are very upset. This is their home and they will have to move. In hopes of stopping the sale, they file a case with a **mediator**. The landlord and tenants have 10 days to **compile** their arguments before **mediation**. What do you think the landlord's statements will be? What do you think the tenants' statements will be?

B. Divide students into two teams. Assign one team to consider the landlord's point of view. The other team should consider the tenants' viewpoints.

C. Ask each team to brainstorm several possible arguments for their viewpoints. Then ask each team to write a one-paragraph opening statement to be read before the mediator.

D. Have teams sit across from each other. Ask one student from each team to present the team's **opening statement**.

E. Invite the landlord's team to begin the mediation by presenting one argument for the sale of the building. The tenant team should answer with a statement that **counters** the argument. Then the tenant team should present an argument to save the building.

F. Continue in this manner until all arguments have been made. Ask students if they think their cultural and personal backgrounds affected their view on this issue. Have them explain.

Closure

Guide students to consider the arguments for both sides. Then ask them to **evaluate** all arguments and come to a **consensus** about the future of the apartment building. Have them complete an Agree/Disagree Matrix. Have students use the Evaluation Rubric on Attachment 1, the Presentation Rubric on Attachment 4, or create a rubric using the Blank Evaluation Rubric on Attachment 3, by which this assignment can be evaluated.

> **Teacher Tip**
>
> **Agree/Disagree Matrix:** Students are polled for agreement or disagreement with a statement and their responses as a group are recorded in the matrix. Students research the topic, and again their responses are recorded. Finally, small groups meet to discuss the results and changes.

Extensions

A. Pose the following questions: Would it have made a difference if there were only four tenants in the entire building? Would it have made a difference if the building were being torn down to build a new city park with a playground, a pond, and large trees? Explain.

B. Ask students to investigate the following:

Compare local rents for apartments in your community versus the purchase payment each month on a mortgage. Use one of the many mortgage payment calculators found on the Internet. Which payment tends to be less expensive and makes for a better use of your money?

Assessment

Use the rubric created or selected by the students to assess the Closure Activity.

Notes

Activity 5 - Discover Child Labor Laws

Differentiation Strategies

Analysis and Synthesis
- Problem Defining
- Evaluation
- Generalizations
- Trend Extrapolation

Ethics/Unanswered Questions
- Problem Sensitivity
- Provocative Questions

Methodology and Use of Resources
- Research
- Note Taking

Enduring Understanding
Society's viewpoints may change over time.

Guiding Questions
(F) What is trend extrapolation?
(F) What is an inference?
(C) Why were child labor laws created by the government?
(C) How did peoples' perspectives changed concerning child labor from the early 1800's to the early 1900's?

Instructional Materials
- computer with Internet access
- books, videos, and other sources about child labor laws

Background Information

In the 1800s, the perspective of children in this country was very different than it is today. People who lived in **rural** America had many children. The children were necessary to help with the chores around the farm. People in **urban** America also had many children. They sent their children to work in factories in order to have enough money to support their families. Children were forced to work long hours in the factories, sometimes 12-15 hours a day. Finally someone realized that this was not safe or **developmentally appropriate**. The government began to create child labor laws. Today child labor laws are very strict in America. However, in many countries children are still forced to work long hours for little pay.

Futurists tell us about the importance of **forecasting** the future. **Trend extrapolation** (**trends** extended into the future and used for **predictions**) is a strategy that combines past events, present events, and creative thinking to forecast future trends. Be sure students understand the terms *trend, extrapolation, forecast,* and *prediction*.

This would be a good time to use a tiered activity. Create packets of printed materials and a list of suggested Web sites on child labor laws in varying degrees of difficulty. Group one may work on child labor laws in the 1800s (this might have the most basic reading assignment), group two may work on the 1900s and have a medium level of difficulty while group three will have the most challenging assignment to research child labor laws of today.

© **Prufrock Press Inc.**

All students are required to take notes on essential information in the packet. Some students should be provided a note taking matrix to guide their work while others take notes on key information from step C.

Group 1 will be asked to create a television ad that will serve as a "teaser" for an up coming after school special on child labor laws of the 1800s.

Group 2 will be asked to create a survey on what students know about child labor laws then choose a way to report the findings to the group.

Group 3 will write a position paper on today's child labor laws and organize a debate.

There is no magic number of versions or tiers.

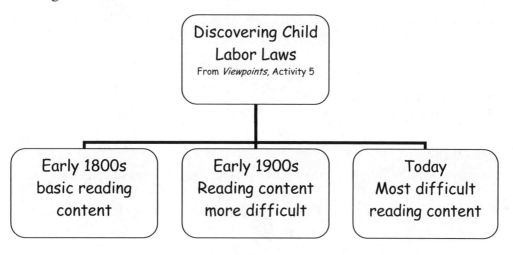

A. Pose the following question: How have child labor laws changed over the past 200 years? Have students form three groups. Designate one of these time periods to each group: early 1800s, early 1900s, and today.

B. Have students research and compare child labor laws in the early 1800s, early 1900s, and today. Allow students to use the Internet, library, videos, and other sources. Have them write generalizations about the information they have discovered. Use the Generalization Rubric on Attachment 5 to guide students in this activity.

C. Have students compile information into reports. Each report should include the following:
- a general overview of the perspective of child labor at that time
- the kinds of labor performed by children at that time
- a summary of some of the laws (if any) in place to protect children at that time

D. Have students use the Presentation Rubric on Attachment 4 or create a rubric by which this assignment will be assessed.

Closure

Instruct each group to present its findings.

Extensions

A. Have students use the information gathered to create a time line of child labor laws. After students present the time line, share the Background Information on trend extrapolation and ask students if they can infer or predict future trends in the laws involving child labor.

B. Pose the following question for discussion: Have child labor laws made things easier or harder for children in America today? Then discuss child labor that still goes on in other countries.

C. Ask students to discuss, graph, and compare different sets of data about student height, weight and ages during the early years of children working in factories. Ask the following questions:
- How would these graphs look today?
- How are the numbers different?
- Can we show the difference graphically? How?

Assessment

Use the rubric created by the students to evaluate the Closure activity.

Notes

Activity 6 – A Dragonfly's Point of View

Differentiation Strategies
Innovation and Application
- Visualization
- Extend Boundaries

Analysis and Synthesis
- Creative Problem Solving
- Inferences

Multiple Perspectives
- Point of View
- Simulation

Enduring Understanding
Viewpoints are rarely stagnant.

Guiding Questions
(F) What are compound eyes?
(F) What types of animals have compound eyes?
(C) How would compound eyes make your life more difficult?

Instructional Materials
- resources with information about compound eyes
- egg cartons (bottoms only; paper cartons work best)
- chenille stems (pipe cleaners)
- tape
- plastic straws
- scissors

Background Information
Insects have eyes, but they cannot see as clearly as people can. Insects may have simple eyes (fleas), compound eyes (dragonflies), or both (grasshoppers). A **simple eye** contains only one lens so the object that the insect sees appears as a single image.

A compound eye is more complex than a simple eye because it is made up of many individual lenses. Compound eyes are like eyes with thousands of tiny eyeballs inside them. Each of these tiny eyeballs is **hexagon** shaped. The hexagon shape helps the tiny eyes fit together in a **spherical** shape. The tiny eyes that make up a compound eye are called **ommatidia**.

A. Have students research the type of eyes insects have, specifically dragonflies. Students will discover that dragonflies have compound eyes (see Background Information.)

B. Have students make a model of a compound eye so they will have an opportunity to see the view through the eyes of a dragonfly. See Dragonfly Eyes on Attachment 6 for directions.

C. After completing the model ask students to draw a representation of what they think a dragonfly eye would look like under a microscope.

D. Choose an object to place in the center of the room. Ask students to draw a picture of the object from a dragonfly's point of view.

E. Have students test their peripheral vision with compound eyes. While one student faces forward, another student stands behind him/her and waves a pencil. The student in front moves only his/her eyes to detect this motion. The student in back slowly moves a pencil out to the side. Where can the motion be detected? Repeat for both sides. Ask: How does that compare to your peripheral vision without the compound eyeglasses?

Closure
Have students write a composition on what they think it would be like if humans had compound eyes. Review the Evaluation Rubric on Attachment 1 or create a rubric for this assignment.

Extensions
A. Ask the following question: Do you think dragonflies think it is difficult to have compound eyes? Guide students to discuss that whatever we are born with is what we are used to. People who are born blind do not know what it is like to see. People who are born deaf do not know what it is like to hear. Everyone adapts to his or her own situation. Discuss how suddenly developing compound eyes would be like suddenly losing one's sight.

B. Invite students to explore the following Web site. As always, please preview all sites before allowing student access.
http://cvs.anu.edu.au/andy/beye/beyehome.html
This site allows students to see through the eyes of a bee. Ask students if there are any other shapes that will work to create a compound eye? Have them draw examples.

C. Have students develop more experiments to do with the compound eye models.

Assessment
Use the rubric selected by the students to assess the Closure activity.

Activity 7 – Memory Power

Differentiation Strategies
Analysis and Synthesis
- Analogies
- Evaluate Situations

Ethics/Unanswered Questions
- Tolerance for Ambiguity
- Provocative Questions

Relevance and Significance
- Role Playing
- Simulation

Enduring Understanding
Viewpoints are rarely stagnant.

Guiding Question
(F) What is a photographic memory?

Instructional Materials
- Optional: transparency and/or copies of Attachment 7

Background Information
These activities encourage students to develop the impression you have a photographic memory. In actuality, you are using mental math tricks to remember a series of numbers. (Do not share this information with students.) Simply allow the students to have their own opinions about whether you have a photographic memory.

A. Begin by telling students a story. Tell them you grew up in a city where everyone thought you had a **photographic memory**, especially with numbers. Explain that everyone was amazed that you could look at a series of numbers and remember most of them at will.

B. Ask for a volunteer to write an 8-digit number on a piece of paper. Have the volunteer show the class or tell the class the number, then allow you to look over the number. However, do not try to memorize the number, simply mentally add each digit together. For example, if the number is 48753297, add $4 + 8 + 7 + 5 + 3 + 2 + 9 + 7 = 45$. Reduce the two-digit number 45 to $4 + 5 = 9$. Remember the 9, and hand the 8-digit number back to the volunteer.

C. Turn your back and have the volunteer circle one digit. Then tell the volunteer to slowly read all of the digits except the one that was circled. Instruct the volunteer to read very slowly because you must concentrate and retrieve the photograph of the numbers from your mind. As the numbers are read, add each number together. Using the previous example, if 4873297 were read, you would add: $4 + 8 + 7 + 3 + 2 + 9 + 7 = 40$. You reduce the answer to a single digit: $4 + 0 = 4$, and then subtract 4 from 9, the number you were supposed to remember. This gives you the number 5, the digit that was circled.

Note
Suppose the 8-digit number was 78579958, which totals 58. $5 + 8 = 13$, which is still a 2-digit number. Add the $1 + 3$, for a total of 4, and remember the 4. Suppose that the volunteer circles that number 5, so he reads $7 + 8 + 7 + 9 + 9 + 5 + 8 = 53$. You reduce the answer to $5 + 3 = 8$. Next, you must subtract the 8 from the 4, which you cannot do. So add 9 to 4 for a total of 13, and then subtract the 8, for an answer of 5.

D. Perform the trick as many times as necessary to give the perception that you have a photographic memory. Discuss what having a photographic memory really means, and whether students believe you have one. Tell them that the answer will be revealed at the end of the curriculum.

Closure
A. Working as partners or teams, have students try out their photographic memories using the 8-digit number trick. Do not give any indication that you do not really have a photographic memory, and do not reveal how to solve the trick. If necessary, hint that mental math might be a useful tool to use if someone just cannot "take a picture" of numbers. Do not tell them that you used math, though.

B. Challenge students to problem-solve how to approach this kind of a trick if they do not actually have a photographic memory. Some students may determine their own mathematical ways to play the trick, and some will come away with the perception that you truly do have a photographic memory.

Extensions
A. Challenge students to develop the hardest numbers they can to test your memory, or to test other students' memories, using this activity.

B. Share the transparency or copies of Attachment 7 with students, challenging them to use their memory powers and photographic memories to memorize or take a picture of the series of numbers.
- Turn your back to the transparency and use your "photographic memory" to answer questions posed by students. Have them ask you to tell all of the digits on a particular line.
- Each line contains 18 digits. The trick is using the number of the line. If the number of the line is even, then add 4 to that number to get the first digit in the line. If the line number is odd, add 9 to the line number to get the first digit in the line.
- Once you have the first digit, then each subsequent digit totals the two previous digits. For example, if the line number is 3, then it is odd; so add $3 + 9 = 12$. The first digit in the line is 2 because you can only use one digit, which is always the second digit of a numeral. The second digit in the line is formed by adding $3 + 2 = 5$. The third digit is formed by adding $2 + 5 = 7$, and so on for 18 digits (not counting the line number). Use a sheet of paper to track the digits as you "remember" them until you have marked off 18 digits.

Note

For a two-digit line number, you again decide to add either 4 or 9, based on even or odd properties. For example, line 18 is even, so you would add 4. 18 + 4 = 22. The first digit in the line is 2. However, because the line number is a two-digit number, to get the next digit you must add the two digits of the line number (1 + 8 = 9). Add 9 to the value of the first digit (9 + 2 = 11). You use the second digit of the numeral (1) as the third digit on the line, and then continue as above.

C. Tell students that this extension actually has a trick to it. Tell them that tricks are developed because not all people have great memories. Have students form teams and give each team a copy of Attachment 7. Ask each team to try to discover the trick, or pattern, in the numbers. Have them present their findings to the class.

D. Use this activity on March 14 every year for Pi Day. (March 14 is 3-14) Ask students to hand calculate 22/7 to get a rough estimate for Pi. Challenge students to calculate and memorize as many digits to Pi as possible. Offer a prize to the student who can memorize Pi to the smallest digit. Here are a few digits of Pi:

3.1415926535 8979323846 2643383279 5028841971 6939937510

Assessment

Assess the level of understanding displayed during the Closure activity.

Notes

Activity 8 – Changing Viewpoints

Differentiation Strategies
Knowledge and Skills
- Categorizing
- Attributes

Innovation and Application
- Visualization
- Extend Boundaries

Ethics/Unanswered Questions
- Provocative Questions
- Problem Sensitivity

Enduring Understanding
Society's viewpoints may change over time.

Guiding Question
(C) How does age change your viewpoint?

Instructional Materials
Back to the Future movie

Preparation
Preview the movie *Back to the Future* and find one or two examples of when Marty goes back in time and sees his parents as they were at his age. Obtain permission from your principal to show portions of the movie to set the stage for this activity.

A. Ask the following question: Do viewpoints change as we get older? Have students explain a situation when they changed their point of view about something as they grew. For example, vacuuming may once have looked fun but now it is a task that is done without the same mystery or enthusiasm.

B. Ask students to imagine their grandparents, parents, aunts, uncles, at several different **stages** in their lives. Show the portions of the *Back to the Future* movie you selected during Preparation. Have them discuss Marty's reaction to seeing his parents acting his age. Have students try to visualize one of their older relatives as they might have been. Have them share their thoughts.

C. Have students brainstorm a time when they said, "When I grow up I'm never going to …" then have students list topics that lend themselves to changing viewpoints as they mature. For example: Napping
- How did you feel about napping when you were very young?
- How do teens feel about naps?
- How do grandparents feel about naps?
- What other topics come to mind that will have changing viewpoints throughout the years?

D. Ask students to imagine themselves at several different stages in their lives. Have them illustrate this progression and use cartoon balloons to show what they are thinking about a certain topic as they mature.

Closure
Have students write a paragraph expressing what they learned about changing viewpoints. Have students create a rubric by which this activity will be assessed.

Extensions
A. Have students ask older family members what they were like at their age and if their point of view has changed over time.

B. Have students create generalizations they can make after completing this lesson. Use the generalization rubric on Attachment 5 to guide in this assignment.

Assessments
Evaluate the Closure activity using the rubric that was selected or created by students.

Notes

_____

_____

_____

_____

_____

_____

_____

_____

_____

_____

_____

_____

_____

Activity 9 – It's Debatable

Differentiation Strategies
Knowledge and Skills
- Classifying
- Research

Multiple Perspectives
- Debate
- Brainstorming
- Inquiry

Enduring Understanding
Viewpoints are rarely stagnant.

Guiding Questions
(F) What is a debate?
(C) How are debates and viewpoints related?

Instructional Materials
- a high school debate team, or a VCR and videotape of a debate
- chart paper
- copies of Attachment 8

A. Tell students they will learn the art of debate. Have students read Attachment 8 to understand the debate process and judging criteria.

B. Have students brainstorm a list of current conflicts in their school, community, country, or world that could be possible debate topics.

C. After the list has been compiled have students, through discussion, eliminate topics they have little or no interest in, have no clear cut points of view, or you deem inappropriate or too sensitive for this age or community. (You should have one topic for every 8 students.)

D. Group students into teams of four. The pro, **affirmative** teams, will argue in support of the topic. Con, or **negative** teams, will argue against the topic.

E. Ask students to complete the research necessary to prepare for the debate. Remind students to use resource people (librarian, principal, other teachers, and parents) to help with their research. Teams should research and develop **statements** and **arguments**.

F. When teams are prepared, hold the debate. Students not debating can be judges. Have them create a judge's record sheet as seen on Attachment 8.

Teacher Tip
Invite a high school debate team to tell your class about and model the steps in a **debate**, or use a videotape of a debate. Ask students to take notes.

G. After the debate lead the following discussion about the debate process. Ask the following to encourage discussion:

- How did you feel about the topic you selected?
- How did you feel about the preparation for the debate?
- Is the debate process fair? If you were going to change something about the debate process, what would it be and why?

Closure

Ask the following question: How are debates and viewpoints related? Challenge students to write essays telling how debates and viewpoints are related. Have students create a scoring rubric for their essays before they begin writing.

Extensions

Ask the following question: What are some viewpoints in U.S. history that have not changed over the past 50 years? (Possible response: children should be educated, children should have earlier bedtimes than adults, etc.) Divide students into four groups and have them list their brainstormed ideas on chart paper. Have teams present arguments and come to a consensus about whether the viewpoint has changed.

Assessment

Use the judge's recording sheets to help assess the debate.

Notes

_____

_____

_____

_____

_____

_____

_____

_____

_____

_____

_____

Differentiation Strategies

Analysis and Synthesis
- Evaluate Situations
- Critical Thinking
- Creative Problem Solving

Ethics/Unanswered Questions
- Evaluate Situations
- Problem Defining
- Provocative Questions

Enduring Understanding
Viewpoints may be manipulated by outside influences.

Guiding Questions
(F) What are statistics?
(C) How can data in graphs be misleading?

Background Information

Different **scales** in graphs can create misleading visual impressions. Many companies that report **statistics** use these "tricks" to make the data appear a certain way in order to influence the point of view of the customer. Bar graphs can be misleading when the vertical scales are broken. The following two graphs present the same information but give two different impressions. The second graph is called a **misleading graph**.

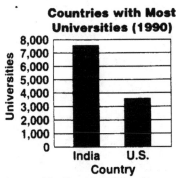

Source: *The Top 10 of Everything.*

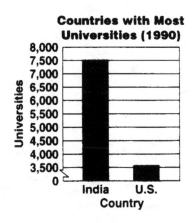

A. Inform students that companies can construct data in a way that shapes viewers' point of view. Re-create the previous graphs on the board or overhead. First show only the second graph. Discuss the information the graph is portraying, and the impression that the students have regarding the information. (It appears that India has almost eight times more universities than the United States.) Then show the first graph. Have students compare the viewpoint they have now with their original viewpoint – knowing that the graph shows the exact same statistics, but portrayed differently.

B. Explain that graphs can give misleading visual impressions. Point out that the **squiggly line**, shown on the second graph, is one way a graph can be misleading. Though it is OK to use the squiggly line, or **break symbol**, to show that some of the values have been left off, this often presents a very misleading impression.

Closure

A. Share the following information with students. Divide students into teams and have each team create an accurate graph and a misleading graph using the same information. On the misleading graph, have students identify exactly what perspective they want the customer to have. (Do they want the customer to think the store sold lots of books? Do they want the customer to think the store did not sell enough books? etc.)

Number of Books Sold Annually at Lily's Bookshop

Year	2000	2001	2002	2003	2004
Books (in millions)	2,005	2,040	2,041	2,079	2,127

B. Have the teams present their graphs without telling the class what is misleading. Ask the class to determine if a graph is misleading and why. Then ask what perception the graph's designer was trying to encourage. Create a rubric by which this assignment will be assessed.

C. Have students create generalizations that can be made about this topic.

Extension

Have students find graphs in magazines and newspapers. If the graph is misleading, have them explain why and then redraw it so it presents an accurate impression of the data. If it is not misleading, have students redraw it and make it misleading. Students should explain the perspective, or impression, a person would get from reading this graph.

Assessment

A. Evaluate the Closure activity and the products using the rubric created by the students.

B. Assess generalizations from the Closure activity using the rubric on Attachment 5.

Differentiation Strategies

Analysis and Synthesis

- Attributes
- Categorization

Analysis and Synthesis

- Evaluate Situations
- Creative Problem Solving

Multiple Perspectives

- Point of View
- Paradoxes

Enduring Understanding

Personal viewpoints may be influenced by a person's culture and/or background.

Guiding Questions

(F) What does it mean to be "rich?"
(F) What is an inference?

A. Read the following story aloud.

> There was once a very wealthy family who lived in Los Angeles, California. The children had never gone without anything they desired. Their mother decided to take them to the country to see how the "poor people" lived. She wanted her children to understand just how lucky they were and to appreciate what they had.
>
> The mother made arrangements with some people in the country, then she and the children stayed with the family for a few days.
>
> As she and the children were driving back to the city and their **opulent** home, she asked, "How was this trip?"
>
> The children talked about how much they enjoyed the trip. Then the mother asked, "Isn't it amazing just how 'poor' people can be?" And the children answered that it was amazing.
>
> Then the mother asked what the children learned from the trip. The children made the following observations:

- They noticed that their own house had a yard with a fence, but the country people had a yard that went on forever.

- They noticed that they had a **chlorinated** swimming pool, but the country people had a river that led into a large, cool lake.

- They noticed that they had floodlights to light their yard at night, but the country people had all the stars in the sky for their lights.

- They noticed that they buy food at the grocery store, but the country people grew their own food.

- They noticed that their house had burglar alarms to protect them, but the country people had their friends and neighbors to protect them.

The children concluded that they were actually the ones who were poor. The country people were truly rich.

The mother did not know what to say.

B. Discuss the two points of view in this story. Whose point of view was correct? Is there a right or wrong viewpoint?

Closure
Discuss the different viewpoints and meanings for the word *rich.* Have children write to the following prompt: How are you rich? Have students create a rubric to assess this assignment.

Extensions
A. Have students solve the perspective mystery on Attachment 9. (The story was about a dog whose food was taken by ants. The ants were then sprayed by the dog's owner.) Students may have other scenarios that fit the paragraph.

B. Invite students to work as partners to write their own perspective mystery. All the characters should be **inferred** but never mentioned. Many adjectives are used to describe what they are doing without telling.

C. Have students create generalizations that can be made about this topic.

Assessment
Use the rubric created by the students to evaluate the Closure Activity.

Activity 12 – It's Magic!

Differentiation Strategies
Analysis and Synthesis
- Analogies
- Evaluate Situations
- Critical Thinking

Ethics/Unanswered Questions
- Problem Defining
- Provocative Questions

Communication
- Research
- Demonstration

Enduring Understanding
Personal viewpoints may be influenced by a person's culture and/or background.

Guiding Questions
(F) What is an illusion?
(C) How are tricks, math, and magic related?

Instructional Materials
- transparency and/or copies of Attachments 10, 11, and 12
- computer with Internet access
- books and videos showing optical illusions
- notebook paper
- transparency markers

Background Information
Many tricks appear to be magic, though they are actually performed using properties of numbers. In some tricks, the use of numbers is not even suspected. The trick to making feats appear to be magic is to keep up a constant "magical" chatter throughout the feat, so spectators do not have time to do too much analysis. For example, say things about certain numbers or items having magical qualities. (i.e. number seven is considered lucky and 13 is considered unlucky) The purpose of this "math magic" trick is to demonstrate that although students may see things that appear to be magic, they are more than likely seeing tricks of mathematics or science.

Illusions are tricks of the mind. These tricks are played on the senses. There are many kinds of illusions. When we think of illusions, pictures of magicians come to mind. During this activity, students can explore the various forms of illusions.

A. Place Attachment 10 on the overhead. Have each student copy the drawing, or make copies of the attachment for each student. Share that you will choose numbers for some of the diamonds and they will choose numbers for some of the diamonds. All of these numbers will determine a magical sum.

B. Tell students to each choose a two-digit number and write it in the first diamond. Ask for three or four volunteers to share their numbers with the class. Record the information on a chart similar to the following.

Student	Diamond 1	Magical Sum

C. Announce that by using your well-developed magical skills, you can determine what the magical sum will be for the 7 diamonds just by knowing the 2-digit number in the first diamond. Mentally add 300 to each two-digit number listed as the first diamond on the previous chart and subtract 3. Record this sum in the chart as the *magical sum*. For example, if a student chooses the number 78 for the first diamond, the magical sum is $78 + 300 - 3 = 375$. For true magical effect, pretend to close your eyes and say *presto* or some other magical word before writing each magical sum on the chart. Tell students that you can determine the magical sum before all of the other numbers are written in the diamonds.

D. Choose one of the two-digit numbers from the chart and write it in the box on the transparency for diamond 1. Then ask for a volunteer to create a different two-digit number, and write that number on the transparency for diamond 2. Have all students also write the numbers for diamond 1 and diamond 2 on their notebook drawings or their attachment copies.

E. You must choose the two-digit number for diamond 3. Mentally subtract the number in diamond 2 from 99. Again, be dramatic and pretend that magic is sending you information, then write the number on the transparency for diamond 3. Have all students copy this number onto their drawings or copies.

F. For diamond 4, have a student volunteer a two-digit number and write it on the transparency. Have students also copy the number. You choose the two-digit number for diamond 5, again by subtracting the number in diamond 4 from 99. Write the new number on the transparency, emphasizing the "magic" of it all. Continue the same process for diamond 6 (student choice) and diamond 7 (your choice to subtract diamond 6 from 99). Then tell each student to add up all seven diamonds to determine if your magical prediction was correct. (Your magical sum on the chart should match your answer on the transparency.)

G. Erase the transparency and repeat the process, choosing one of the other 3 numbers from the chart as the first diamond. <u>Do not</u> have students erase their drawings or copies. Have them keep the first one, and then draw an additional drawing. On the new drawing, have all students write the same numbers on their drawings as you do it on the board. Again, it will prove that your magical prediction was correct. Do not forget to use magical language and gestures as you perform the trick.

Diamond 1 – choose a two-digit number from the chart
Diamond 2 – have a student choose a two-digit number
Diamond 3 – you choose a two-digit number by subtracting diamond 2 from 99
Diamond 4 – have a student choose a two-digit number
Diamond 5 – you choose a two-digit number by subtracting diamond 4 from 99
Diamond 6 – have a student choose a two-digit number
Diamond 7 – you choose a two-digit number by subtracting diamond 6 from 99
Then add all of the diamonds together to get the magical sum.

H. Discuss the perception that this is true magic. (From the students' viewpoint, the trick appears to be magic. From the teacher's viewpoint, the trick is just mathematics.)

I. Ask the students to work in groups to investigate the mathematics behind this trick, using their two drawings or copies. Students will probably use the problem solving strategy of **guess, check, and revise**. They should form an educated guess, check or test the guess, and then revise as necessary until they reach an answer. If necessary, perform the trick a few more times to add examples to the chart.

J. Share the hint that students should look at the last two digits of the magical sum. Students should discover the pattern is that the last two digits of the magical sum form a number that is 3 less than the number in diamond 1. They should discover that the sum of diamonds 2 and 3, 4 and 5, and 6 and 7 is each 99. Therefore, the rule of the trick is diamond 1 + 99 + 99 + 99 = magical sum, or diamond 1 + 300 − 3 = magical sum.

Closure
A. Have students form teams and work together to create a mathematical pattern that can be developed into a magic trick.

B. Have each team perform the tricks for the class, emphasizing that they must each work hard at making the trick appear to be a true magical trick, or creating a magical perspective for the audience.

C. Invite the class to discover the mathematics behind the magical math tricks. Have students create a rubric by which this activity will be assessed.

Extensions

A. Have each team perform its magical trick for another class. Another possibility is for the class to put on a mathematical magic show for the school. Performances can be videotaped.

B. Share the second paragraph of the Background Information on Optical Illusions. Have students complete the Optical Illusions independent activity on Attachment 11.

C. Share the following scenario with students:

> Five of the world's best bakers met in London to **compete** in a bake-off to determine the best baker. The grand prizewinner would earn the title of World's Best Baker. The bakers agreed to use the same ingredients in their apple pies. However, each baker was from a different part of the world. Because their cultures were so different, each had a different perspective of how much of each ingredient truly made a great apple pie. They just could not agree on how many apples should be in the pie, nor could they agree about the amount of time an apple pie should be baked.

D. Use Attachment 12 as a transparency. Read the clues with students to determine the full name of each baker, the amount of apples he or she used in the apple pie, and the amount of time to bake the apple pie. Fill in both charts as information is discovered. Both charts are needed to solve the puzzle.

Answers:
- Olga Sovinsky uses 8 apples and bakes her pie for 16 minutes and 9 seconds.
- Haas Hand uses 5 apples and bakes his pie for 16 minutes and 17 seconds.
- Su Lang uses 9 apples and bakes his pie for 17 minutes.
- Nancy Smith uses 7 apples and bakes her pie for 17 minutes and 7 seconds.
- Maria Hernandez uses 10 apples and bakes her pie for 17 minutes and 8 seconds.

E. Ask students to work in teams to create their own logic puzzles. Have them switch puzzles with other teams and solve.

F. Use apple pies to review fractions of a circle. Ask: If we have half an apple pie and we take away one quarter of the pie, how much of the apple pie will be left? (answer: one quarter) Point out that students are subtracting fractions with unlike denominators. Develop similar questions to challenge students.

Assessment
Use the rubric created by the students to evaluate the closure activity.

Notes

_____

_____

_____

_____

_____

_____

_____

_____

_____

_____

_____

_____

_____

_____

_____

_____

_____

_____

_____

_____

Activity 13 – Another Meaning

Differentiation Strategies
Knowledge and Skills
- Visualization
- Demonstration

Innovation and Application
- Extend Boundaries
- Analogical Thinking

Analysis and Synthesis
- Draw Conclusions
- Convergent and Divergent Thinking

Communication
- Research
- Writing Skills

Instructional Materials
- computer with Internet access
- *If...* book, by Sarah Perry

Enduring Understanding
Personal viewpoints may be influenced by a person's culture and/or background.

Guiding Questions
(F) What is an idiom?
(C) How can idioms be confusing?

Background Information
Idioms are sayings that cannot be understood using the **literal** meaning of the words. We use **idiomatic expressions** to paint a more colorful picture of an event we are describing.

A. Explain that we use idiomatic expressions when we are speaking and writing informally to paint a more vivid picture of the story we are telling.

B. Ask students to imagine the following situation:

A group of foreign exchange students from Japan just arrived in America. The students are meeting with their main host before meeting their families. The host has the following speech prepared:

> Welcome students. I understand <u>the last leg of your trip</u> was difficult. The next part <u>will be a breeze</u> compared to your flight.
>
> If you're nervous about <u>hooking up</u> with your host families, <u>don't sweat it</u>. Most of the families have had foreign exchange students before, <u>so they know the ropes</u>. They are

on cloud nine because you're here. All of the families <u>will</u>
<u>bend over backward</u> to make sure you're <u>cracking smiles</u>
before the end of the day.

Here are a few reminders before you meet your families.
First, I realize you will be <u>struggling to make ends meet</u>, but
we're taking a trip to New York City later this fall, so save
your money.
Have a great time in America, students. I'll <u>be in touch</u> soon.

C. Discuss the idiomatic expressions in the story. Which phrases would probably be hard for foreign exchange students to understand? Reread the story and have students change the idioms to words that a foreign exchange student would understand.

D. Ask students to imagine what the foreign exchange students were picturing in their minds as they listened to the host. Go through each idiomatic expression and have students discuss their **literal visualizations**.

E. Have students brainstorm other idiomatic expressions. Some more familiar idiomatic expressions include: cat got your tongue, wet behind the ears, plain as the nose on your face, paid through the nose, drop me a line, face the music, and walk the line.

F. Ask each student to choose an idiomatic expression to illustrate. They should include a foreign exchange student in their illustrations as well as a thinking bubble showing what the idiomatic expression conveyed to the student. The idiomatic expression should be written at the bottom of the picture. Create a rubric by which this assignment can be assessed.

Closure
Have each student present his or her idiomatic expression. Discuss how idiomatic expressions relate to perspectives.

Extensions
A. Have students discuss what they can do the next time they meet a student who has not mastered American idiomatic expressions.

B. Have students visit the below Web sites containing idioms. As always, please preview all sites before allowing students to access them.
http://home.t-online.de/home/toni.goeller/idiom_wm/
http://www.doghause.com/idioms.html
http://www.linguarama.com/ps/295-6.htm

C. Read the book *If. . .* then answer the following questions:
- Why do you think the author/illustrator combined the things she did?
- Choose one page from the book and create text for the page.

- Brainstorm all the possibilities of the chosen illustrations. Then compose an essay beginning with: If _____ were/had _____ . . .
- Share with the class the illustrations and text you composed.
- Combine two pictures and verbally tell a story. For example, if cats could fly and dogs were mountains, what would happen?

Assessment

Evaluate the illustrated idiomatic expression product in step F using the rubric created by the students.

Notes

_____

_____

_____

_____

_____

_____

_____

_____

_____

_____

_____

_____

_____

_____

_____

_____

_____

_____

_____

_____

_____

_____

Activity 14 - Different Values

Differentiation Strategies

Multiple Perspectives
- Paradoxes
- Point of View
- Debate

Ethics/Unanswered Questions
- Provocative Questions
- Tolerance for Ambiguity

Innovation and Application
- Analogical Thinking
- Extend Boundaries

Instructional Materials
- computer with Internet access

> ### Enduring Understanding
> Personal viewpoints may be influenced by a person's culture and/or background.
>
> ### Guiding Questions
> (F) What is a paradox?
> (P) Should animals be held in captivity?

A. Ask students to consider the following question: How is treating circus animals **humanely** a **paradox**?

B. Have students consider the point of view of the circus animal. Ask what they think circus life is like for an elephant, tiger, or a trained horse.

C. Ask students to consider the point of view of the circus trainers and owners. How do they see the lives of the animals that perform in the circus?

D. Invite students to consider the points of view of circus animals, circus owners, and trainers. Have them write an essay telling why their point of view is correct.

E. Have students share their essays with the class.

Closure
Lead a discussion in which the students debate what they think is right. Use the All About Debate guide on Attachment 8.

Extension
Pose the following questions for discussion: Are animals in **captivity** treated humanely? Is captivity humane?

Assessment
Evaluate the debate using the judging criteria on Attachment 8.

Activity 15 – Infant Viewpoints

Differentiation Strategies
Knowledge and Skills
- Attributes
- Classifying
- Categorizing

Methodology and Use of Resources
- Inquiry
- Research

Communication
- Writing Skills
- Uses Technological Media

Instructional Materials
- computer with Internet access

Enduring Understanding
Viewpoints are rarely stagnant.

Guiding Question
(C) How is the development of animals related to their chance of surviving infancy?

A. Discuss the development of human babies. Keep the discussion away from how babies are conceived. Guide the discussion to the development after birth. Ask students to consider the amount of care a human infant needs to survive. Pose the question: Can a human infant survive on its own?

B. Have students form groups of three. Ask them to choose one of the following animals to research: kangaroo, panda, chimpanzee, mouse, rattlesnake, seahorse, horse, or domestic cat.

C. Have each group research the **dependency** stage of each of these animals. They will need to gather information on the following details:
- What are the babies called?
- How big are they when they are born?
- Does the mother or father care for the babies?
- How many babies are born at one time?
- How does the baby survive?
- If the mother or father cares for the babies after birth, what does he or she teach them?

D. Have each group compare the animal to human babies. Which **species** is more likely to survive if left on its own at birth? Which species does a better job caring for its infants?

© Prufrock Press Inc.

43

E. Have each group write a story from the animal's viewpoint. The story should be about the first few hours of life for the creature. What does the animal do? What does it see or hear? Or does it see or hear? Does the animal eat? Have students create a rubric by which this assignment will be assessed.

Closure
Allow time for groups to present their stories to the class. Ask the following closing question: Which animal would you prefer to be and why?

Extensions
A. Have students discuss the **qualities** an animal must have in order to survive on its own after being born. Then have students create a list of animals that do not need a mother when they are born.

B. Have students use the paper pyramid pattern on Attachment 13 to illustrate three stages of life for the animal they researched.

Assessment
Evaluate the story using the rubric that was selected or created by students.

Notes

_____

_____

_____

_____

_____

_____

_____

_____

_____

Activity 16 – Poetry Perspectives

Differentiation Strategies
Analysis and Synthesis
- Aesthetic Thinking
- Critical Thinking

Multiple Perspectives
- Inquiry
- Point of View

Communication
- Decision Making
- Writing Skills

Instructional Materials
- a variety of poetry books

A. Gather a variety of poetry books for students to read. Have students read as partners.

B. Ask students to choose one poem to study. They should answer the following questions about their poems:
- Who are the characters in the poem?
- What is the main idea of the poem?
- From what point of view is the poem written?
- Does the poem rhyme? Where are the rhyming words located?
- How many lines does the poem have?
- What is the **rhythm** of the poem? Where are the **accent** words?

C. Challenge students to rewrite the poem from a different **point of view**. Students must use the same poem format as the original poem. They can rewrite the poem from their own perspective, another character's perspective, or a third person perspective. Have students create a rubric by which this assignment will be assessed.

Dickinson

D. Invite students to illustrate their poems.

Closure
Have students share their new perspective poetry with the class.

Extensions

A. Invite students to choose a favorite fairy tale to rewrite from a different perspective. Students may choose to create a puppet show or play to present to the class. For example, have students rewrite Cinderella from the point of view of one of the stepsisters.

B. Have students complete the Poetry Tic-Tac-Toe on Attachment 14.

Assessment

Evaluate the Closure using the rubric created by the students.

Notes

_____

_____

_____

_____

_____

_____

_____

_____

_____

_____

_____

_____

_____

_____

_____

Differentiation Strategies

Analysis and Synthesis
- Critical Thinking
- Aesthetic Thinking

Multiple Perspectives
- Visual Points of View
- Visualization

Communication
- Art and Geometry Skills
- Research

Instructional Materials
- a variety of art books

Enduring Understanding
Viewpoints are rarely stagnant.

Guiding Question
(C) How can viewpoints be expressed in art?

Background Information
During the **Renaissance Period,** artists became very interested in making two-dimensional artworks look three-dimensional. They used mathematics and close observation to invent **"linear perspective"**—a technique that helps artists make things look deep. Download several of the following examples to share with students. As always, please preview all sites before allowing student access.

http://www.mos.org/sln/Leonardo/ExploringLinearPerspective.html
http://psych.hanover.edu/Krantz/art/linear.html
http://www2.evansville.edu/studiochalkboard/lp-intro.html
http://www.ateliersaintandre.net/en/pages/aesthetics/byzantine_perspective.html

A. Share the Background information and examples of linear perspective. Invite students to look through art books and find examples of two and three-dimensional works.

B. Explain to students that before the Renaissance Period artists did not use perspective in drawings, and art appeared flat. Ask students to find example of art without perspective.

C. Ask students to follow the directions listed below:
- Turn your paper horizontal ("landscape" **orientation**).
- Line the end of your ruler up with the side of your page. Be sure the ruler is straight and flush with the edge of the page or everything will be crooked!
- Draw a horizontal line one or two inches down from top of the page. This is your horizon line.

- Draw a dot in the middle of your horizon line. This is your vanishing point.
- Draw a square or rectangle in the right or left bottom area of your page.
- Connect three corners of your rectangle or square to the vanishing point. These are **orthogonals**.
- Draw a horizontal line between the top two orthogonals where you want your form to end.
- Draw a vertical line down from the horizontal line to complete the side.
- Erase the remaining orthogonals.

D. Ask: Does perspective change the viewpoint of an artist? Does it change the viewpoint of the observer? How do artists see things in different ways?

Closure
Challenge students to apply the use of linear perspective in a simple drawing. Have students create a rubric by which this assignment will be assessed.

Extensions
A. Challenge students to draw their names in linear perspective. Encourage students to add details or create a new picture of a city block, county fair, or the classroom in perspective.

B. Allow students to research artists of the Renaissance Period and discover which ones used perspective in their work.

Assessment
Use the rubric created by the students to assess the Closure activity.

Notes

_____

_____

_____

_____

_____

_____

_____

_____

_____

_____

Activity 18 – Zoom!

Differentiation Strategies

Analysis and Synthesis
- Convergent and Divergent Thinking
- Creative Problem Solving

Ethics/Unanswered Questions
- Provocative Questions
- Aesthetic Thinking

Multiple Perspectives
- Brainstorming
- Group Consensus

Communication
- Decision Making
- Writing Skills

Instructional Materials
- Drawing Materials
- *Zoom* book, by Istvan Banyai

Optional:
Rezoom book, by Istvan Banyai

Enduring Understanding
Personal viewpoints may be influenced by a person's culture and/or background.

Guiding Question
(C) Can only viewing a portion of an object or understanding a portion of a concept skew your point of view?

A. Show the book *Zoom*. Ask students to make predictions about the book.

B. Turn to the first page. Allow time for students to determine what they are seeing.

C. Slowly turn the pages in the rest of the book. Allow time for students to make predictions about the next point of view to be shown. When you get to the middle of the book, have students predict what they think will be the last picture in the book.

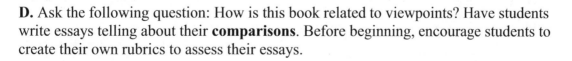

D. Ask the following question: How is this book related to viewpoints? Have students write essays telling about their **comparisons**. Before beginning, encourage students to create their own rubrics to assess their essays.

E. Have the class form two teams. Challenge the teams to create their own versions of the *Zoom* book using the following steps.
- Meet as a team to determine the point of view for each picture.
- Assign pictures to be drawn by each team member.
- Draw a picture and put the book together.
- Create a title page for your book.
- Select a team member to present your book to the class.

Closure
Read the Guiding Question for this lesson and have students respond in essay form. Have students create a rubric by which this assignment will be assessed.

Extensions
A. Ask students if they have ever viewed the world from the perspective or viewpoint of an inanimate object. Share the "true" stories on Attachment 15 then challenge students to work in pairs or small teams to create similar stories that explain a process or teaches a lesson.

B. Invite students to look at *Rezoom* by the author of *Zoom*.

Assessment
A. Evaluate the Closure using the rubric created by the students.

B. Use the rubric created in Step D to assess essays.

Notes

_____

_____

_____

_____

_____

_____

_____

_____

_____

Activity 19 - Post-Assessment

Differentiation Strategies

Knowledge and Skills
- Visualization
- Demonstration

Multiple Perspectives
- Brainstorming
- Point of View

Ethics/Unanswered Questions
- Provocative Questions
- Problem Finding

Instructional Materials
- chart paper

A. Draw the illustration located in Activity 1 on the chalkboard again. Have students brainstorm all the different things the drawing could be. Invite students to share their ideas with the class. Ask students to compare the number of responses generated today to the responses generated during the first activity in *Viewpoints*.

B. Have students illustrate the most important thing they learned during *Viewpoints*.

C. Pose the following question: Do I really have a photographic memory? Ask students to vote and record their responses. Lead a class discussion emphasizing that all of the magic and memory activities done in *Viewpoints* really worked because of mathematical tricks or patterns. Have students create their own mathematical tricks and present them to the class.

Notes

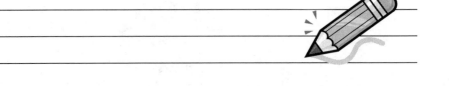

Attachment 1   Evaluation Rubric

Student or Team: _____

Assignment: _____

Directions: Mark the appropriate rating for each criterion. Use these individual ratings to assign an overall rating for the assignment.

RATINGS	0 Working on it!	1 Novice	2 Acceptable	3 Out of the Box!	Not Applicable
Topic	Did not stay on topic	Stayed on topic for most of presentation	Stayed on topic and demonstrated some elaboration	Stayed on topic with extensive elaboration and application	N/A
Oral Expression	Could not express ideas	Could only express some ideas	Easy to understand	Very well articulated	N/A
Organization	Not organized	Was somewhat organized	Very organized	Organization far exceeded the standards	N/A
Written Expression	Could not express ideas in written form	Could only express some ideas	Expressed ideas well	Ideas very well expressed and defined; much elaboration	N/A
OVERALL					

Comments:

Directions: Analyze Black Beauty using DeBono's Six Thinking Hats.

WHITE HAT

List three facts you learned about life during the late 1800s:

1.

2.

3.

BLACK HAT

What emotional problems and feelings did Black Beauty have while coping with various handlers, owners, and situations?

RED HAT

How does Black Beauty feel about racing? What was the alternative?

BLUE HAT

List the things Black Beauty learns to do in order to avoid abuse and survive?

GREEN HAT

What one thing would you have done differently if you had been there in Black Beauty's place?

YELLOW HAT

What do you think people learn from reading this book? What do you think the author was trying to teach us?

Attachment 3   Blank Evaluation Rubric

Student or Team: _____

Assignment: _____

Directions: Mark the appropriate rating for each criterion. Use these individual ratings to assign an overall rating for the assignment.

Criteria	0 Working on it!	1 Novice	2 Acceptable	3 Out of the Box!	Not Applicable
OVERALL					

Comments:

Student or Team: _____

Assignment: _____

Directions: Mark the appropriate rating for each criterion. Use these individual ratings to assign an overall rating for the assignment.

Criteria	0 Working on it!	1 Novice	2 Acceptable	3 Out of the Box!	Not Applicable
Uses Pre-writing strategies	Cannot generate pre-writing graphic organizers, notes, or brain-storming	Some use of pre-writing in the form of organizers, notes, or brainstorming	Use of more than one pre-writing strategy; mostly well organized and thought out	Numerous strategies used and followed to create a well-organized and thought-out composition	N/A
Content is valid and accurate	Content is weak and shows little insight	Content is accurate but lacks insight; few supporting examples	Content is accurate with some questions left unanswered and a few supporting examples	Content is 100 percent accurate and has supporting examples	N/A
Organization	Not organized	Somewhat organized	Very organized	Organization far exceeded the standards	N/A
Oral Presentation of information	Could not express or present information	Presentation lacked creativity and was not very informative	Presentation moderately creative, entertaining, and informative	Engaging presentation that was creative, entertaining, and informative	N/A
OVERALL					

Comments:

Attachment 5 — Generalization Rubric

Student or Team: _____

Assignment: _____

Directions: Mark the appropriate rating for each criterion. Use these individual ratings to assign an overall rating for the assignment.

RATINGS	0 Working on it!	1 Novice	2 Acceptable	3 Out of the Box!
Generalizations	Unable to make a generalization with help	Began to make generalizations between ideas with help	Made simple generalizations with little help	Made complex generalizations between ideas with no help

Extended Skills to Consider:
- making generalizations between two or more disciplines
- extending to apply generalizations to other real-world problems

Comments:

1. Cut out two adjacent egg cups from the egg carton.

2. Cut out a hole about one inch in diameter in the bottom of each cup.

3. Poke two holes in the sides of the frame to form earpieces.

4. Cut four or five straws into four pieces of approximately equal length.

5. Bunch seven or eight of the straw segments into a round bundle.

6. Have one person hold the bunched straws together while another person wraps tape around the straws to hold them all together.

7. Make another bundle exactly the same.

8. Slide the taped bundles into the holes of the frames.

9. Look through the frames to view the world like a dragonfly!

Line
Number

1	0	1	1	2	3	5	8	3	1	4	5	9	4	3	7	0	7	7
2	6	8	4	2	6	8	4	2	6	8	4	2	6	8	4	2	6	8
3	2	5	7	2	9	1	0	1	1	2	3	5	8	3	1	4	5	9
4	8	2	0	2	2	4	6	0	6	6	2	8	0	8	8	6	4	0
5	4	9	3	2	5	7	2	9	1	0	1	1	2	3	5	8	3	1
6	0	6	6	2	8	0	8	8	6	4	0	4	4	8	2	0	2	2
7	6	3	9	2	1	3	4	7	1	8	9	7	6	3	9	2	1	3
8	2	0	2	2	4	6	0	6	6	2	8	0	8	8	6	4	0	4
9	8	7	5	2	7	9	6	5	1	6	7	3	0	3	3	6	9	5
10	4	5	9	4	3	7	0	7	7	4	1	5	6	1	7	8	5	3
11	0	2	2	4	6	0	6	6	2	8	0	8	8	6	4	0	4	4
12	6	9	5	4	9	3	2	5	7	2	9	1	0	1	1	2	3	5
13	2	6	8	4	2	6	8	4	2	6	8	4	2	6	8	4	2	6
14	8	3	1	4	5	9	4	3	7	0	7	7	4	1	5	6	1	7
15	4	0	4	4	8	2	0	2	2	4	6	0	6	6	2	8	0	8
16	0	7	7	4	1	5	6	1	7	8	5	3	8	1	9	0	9	9
17	6	4	0	4	4	8	2	0	2	2	4	6	0	6	6	2	8	0
18	2	1	3	4	7	1	8	9	7	6	3	9	2	1	3	4	7	1
19	8	8	6	4	0	4	4	8	2	0	2	2	4	6	0	6	6	2
20	4	6	0	6	6	2	8	0	8	8	6	4	0	4	4	8	2	0

Room Setup

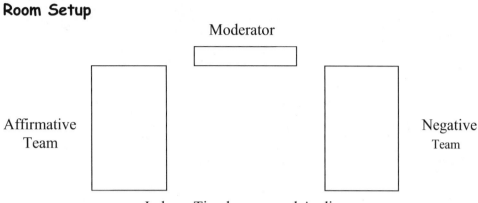

Debate Duties

There are several jobs in a debate. The affirmative team consists of four students who support the topic (or resolution). The negative team also has four members and argues against the resolution.

The moderator keeps the debate moving by directing who will speak next. The timekeeper keeps the time of each speaker and signals the moderator when a person's time is up.

The judges judge the debate based on the arguments presented by both sides. The judges decide which side wins the debate.

Debate Format

Opening Statements – **2 minutes for each team**

There are four speakers for each team. The first speaker on each team makes an opening statement. This statement tells the resolution and the main argument of the team. For example, if the resolution is wearing school uniforms, the affirmative team's statement would say it supports wearing uniforms to school and the negative team's statement would be against wearing school uniforms.

Second and Third Speakers – **2 minutes for each team**

The second and third speakers from each side ask and answer questions during this part of the debate. The affirmative team questions the negative team for 2 minutes and vice versa. Both teams answer the questions the best way they can.

Planning Final Statement – **3 minutes**

Members of each team talk among themselves about the debate so far and plan a closing statement to be delivered by the fourth speaker.

Fourth Speaker – 1 minute each
Fourth speakers for each team deliver closing statements summarizing their main arguments.

Judges' Decision – 3 minutes
The judges meet and discuss the debate. They rate each speaker, decide which team won the debate, then announce the winner.

Sample Judge's Sheet

Rate speakers on a scale of 1 to 4, with 4 being the best.

Affirmative Team

Speaker 1
Did the speaker present the opening statement clearly?
1   2   3   4

Did the speaker speak at a good rate?
1   2   3   4

Was the speaker convincing?
1   2   3   4

Speakers 2 and 3
Did they present questions and answers clearly?
1   2   3   4

Were they convincing?
1   2   3   4

Speaker 4
Was the closing argument well presented?
1   2   3   4

Did the speaker support the closing argument with facts presented during the debate?
1   2   3   4

Negative Team

Speaker 1
Did the speaker present the opening statement clearly?
1   2   3   4

Did the speaker speak at a good rate?
1   2   3   4

Was the speaker convincing?
1   2   3   4

Speakers 2 and 3
Did they present questions and answers clearly?
1   2   3   4

Were they convincing?
1   2   3   4

Speaker 4
Was the closing argument well presented?
1   2   3   4

Did the speaker support the closing argument with facts presented during the debate?
1   2   3   4

Read the following mystery:

> I was lying in the corner, minding my own business when a group of **militant** beings marched in and **pilfered** my food. I observed as they struggled to haul away every **morsel** in the container. Suddenly, someone was standing over the thieves, showering them with a mist. The **riffraff** stopped in their tracks and crumpled to the ground, my food **strewn** across the room.

Answer the following questions:

Who is telling the story?

What is it about?

Who are the characters?

Magical Diamonds

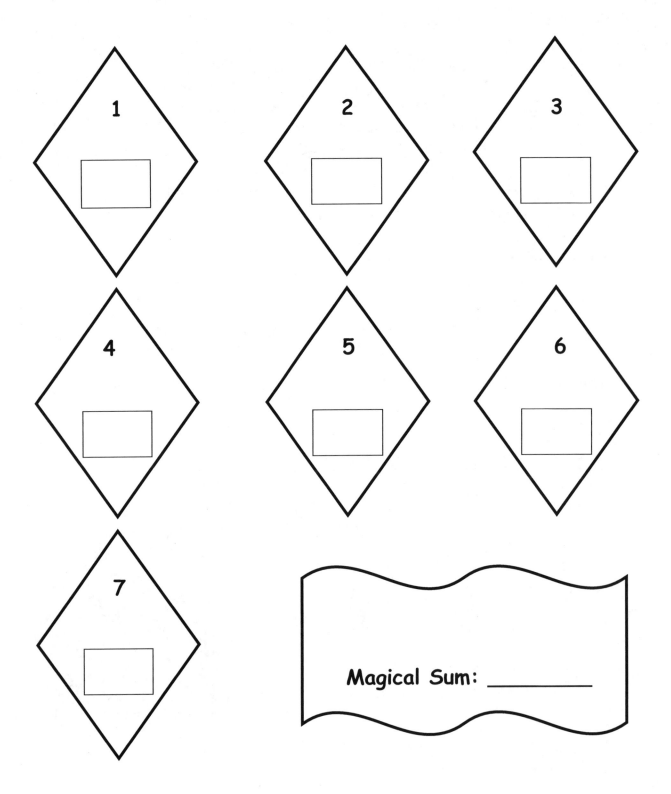

Magical Sum: _____

Attachment 11   Optical Illusions

Instructional Materials
- computer with Internet access
- books and videos showing optical illusions

A. Search the following Web sites to view optical illusions:

http://www.ee.bgu.ac.il/~idog/amazing/
http://www.sandlotscience.com/
http://www.exploratorium.edu/exhibits/f_exhibits.html

B. Working in pairs find an optical illusion you can print out or reproduce and explain how it works.

C. Present your optical illusion to the class.

D. Explain how viewpoints and illusions are related?

BONUS:
Research different types of optical illusions and create a new optical illusion.

1. Ms. Smith bakes her apple pie for 17 minutes and 7 seconds.

2. Mr. Hand uses 2 apples fewer than Nancy, and bakes his pie longer than only one other baker.

3. Mr. Lang, whose first name is not Maria, bakes his pie 51 seconds longer than Olga does, and uses one apple less than Ms. Hernandez.

4. Ms. Sovinsky uses one less apple than Mr. Lang does.

5. Ms. Hernandez uses more apples than Ms. Sovinsky does.

6. Nancy isn't Ms. Hernandez.

7. Ms. Sovinsky bakes for less time than do either Su or Maria.

8. The woman who bakes for 17 minutes 7 seconds uses 7 apples.

9. Maria bakes her pie for 17 minutes 8 seconds, 1 second longer than Nancy does.

10. The person using 5 apples isn't Ms. Sovinsky.

11. Olga bakes her apple pie for the least amount of time, and uses 8 apples.

12. Su has been a baker longer than Mr. Hand.

	First name					Time (minutes/seconds)					Apples				
	Haas	Nancy	Olga	Maria	Su	16m/9s	16m/17s	17m	17m/7s	17m/8s	5	7	8	9	10
Sovinsky															
Lang															
Smith															
Hand															
Hernandez															

First Name	Last Name	Time	Apples
		16m/9s	
		16m/17s	
		17m	
		17m/7s	
		17m/8s	

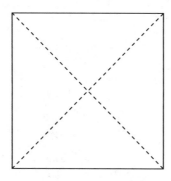

1. Begin with a square piece of paper.

2. Fold the square in half as shown, creating 2 creases.

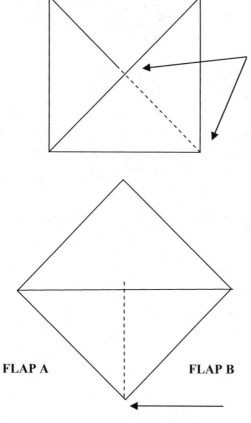

3. Unfold the square and cut from one corner to the center fold.

4. Fold Flap B under Flap A to create a three-dimensional triangular pyramid. Secure with glue or tape.

5. You can create a four-sided pyramid by making 4 paper pyramids and gluing the backsides together.

FLAP A   FLAP B

Complete a tic-tac-toe in any direction by completing three of these activities during independent study. Lightly shade in the boxes as you complete each task.

Research a famous person and write a poem about a significant event that may have changed his or her point of view.	Create a poem that leaves people guessing who is telling the story.	Make a list of twelve topics that could be written about in poetic form that expresses a point of view.
Read a well-known poem that voices a strong point of view and critique it.	Create your own poetry activity!	Select a poem that voices a strong point of view then compose a paragraph telling whether you agree or disagree with the poet's viewpoint.
Select a poem that has a strong point of view then revise it to state just the opposite.	Find and share three poems that show varying degrees of viewpoints. For example, no point of view, moderate point of view, and strong point of view.	Take a survey about a topic that you do not have strong feelings about, then write a poem in support of the majority opinion.

"True" Story # 1
I bang my head on hard objects every day.
People hold me to use me.
I come in a variety of colors and sizes.
I help "drive" objects into other objects.
I am very loud.
I feel cold when you touch me.
I have rubber around the bottom part of me so you can grip me tightly.

What am I?

"True" Story #2

I have a spine.
I can be hard.
People "leaf" through me. This tickles!
Sometimes kids throw me. This hurts!
I can be soft. I can be torn easily.
I don't make noise unless I'm dropped.
There are many different kinds of me; "coloring" and "how-to" are two kinds.

What am I?

"True" Story #3
I make lots of noise!
The noise I make is high-pitched.
I am used by policemen, coaches, band leaders, referees, and many others.
I can be used in games, or just for fun.
You wouldn't want to use me inside a small area. I can hurt your ears!
I am a small, hard object.
I come in many styles and colors.

What am I?

"True" Story #4
I have sharp edges.
I am one thing, but when people talk about me, my name sounds plural.
I can help you wrap a present, open a box, or trim your hair.
I am not a loud object.
I am not a soft object.
I come in many colors and styles.
You should never run with me.

What am I?

Viewpoints
Vocabulary and Materials Checklist

Activity	Vocabulary	Materials Needed
1	viewpoints	chart paper
2	graphic organizer politics racism	drawing materials
3	perspective horse whispering	*Black Beauty* book, by Anna Sewell (matching multiple copies) computer with Internet access
4	compile consensus counters dilapidated evaluate hypothetical landlord mediation mediator opening statement tenants	
5	developmentally appropriate rural urban futurists forecasting prediction trend extrapolation trends	computer and Internet access books, videos, and other sources on child labor laws
6	compound eye hexagon ommatidia spherical	resources with information about compound eyes egg cartons (bottoms only; paper cartons work best) chenille stems (pipe cleaners) tape plastic straws scissors
7	photographic memory	transparency of Attachment 7
8	stages	DVD or video copy of *Back to the Future*
9	affirmative arguments debate negative statements	a high school debate team, or a VCR and videotape of a debate copies of Attachment 8 chart paper

10	break symbol misleading graph scales squiggly line statistics	
11	inferred militant morsel pilfered riffraff strewn chlorinated opulent	
12	illusions compete guess, check and revise	transparency and or copies of Attachments 10, 11, and 12 transparency markers computer with Internet access books and videos showing optical illusions notebook paper
13	idiomatic expressions idioms literal literal visualizations	computer with Internet access *If...*book, by Sarah Perry
14	captivity humanely paradox	computer with Internet access
15	dependency species qualities	computer with Internet access
16	accent point of view rhythm	a variety of poetry books
17	linear perspective orientation orthagonal Renaissance Period	a variety of art books
18		*Zoom* and *Rezoom* books by Istvan Banyai drawing materials
19		chart paper

Note: Paper and pencils should be on-hand each day, as should writing and illustration supplies, and may not be listed on the Checklist.

Viewpoints

Differentiation Strategies and TEKS Checklist

Activity	Differentiation Strategies	TEKS: Language Arts and Reading	TEKS: Mathematics	TEKS: Social Studies	TEKS: Science
1	**Multiple Perspectives** Brainstorming Point of View **Ethics/Unanswered Questions** Provocative Questions Problem Finding	Write to express, discover, record, develop, reflect ideas, and to problem solvers			

Activity	Differentiation Strategies	TEKS: Language Arts and Reading	TEKS: Mathematics	TEKS: Social Studies	TEKS: Science
2	**Knowledge and Skills** Attributes Categorizations **Analysis and Synthesis** Convergent and Divergent Thinking Creative Problem Solving **Ethics/Unanswered Questions** Provocative Questions Aesthetic Thinking **Multiple Perspectives** Brainstorming Group Consensus	Connect his/her own experiences, information, insights, and ideas with those of other through speaking and listening Write to express, discover, record, develop, reflect on ideas, and to problem solve Select, organize, or produce visuals to complement and extend meanings Offer observations, make connections, react, speculate, interpret, and raise questions in response to texts Interpret and evaluate the various ways visual image makers such as graphic artists, illustrators, and news photographers represent meanings	Identify the mathematics in everyday situations	Communicate in written, oral, and visual forms Use problem-solving and decision-making skills	
3	**Knowledge and Skills** Attributes Inferences **Analysis and Synthesis** Analogies Aesthetic Thinking	Analyze characters, including their traits, motivations, conflicts, points of view, relationships, and changes they undergo Describe how the author's perspective or point of	Select or develop an appropriate problem-solving strategy, including drawing a picture, looking for a pattern, systematic guessing and checking, acting it out, making a table, working a simpler problem, or working backwards to solve		

74

Activity	Differentiation Strategies	TEKS: Language Arts and Reading	TEKS: Mathematics	TEKS: Social Studies	TEKS: Science
	Multiple Perspectives Point of View Shared Inquiry	view affects the text Compare text events with his/her own and other readers' experiences Determine distinctive and common characteristics of cultures through wide reading Articulate and discuss themes and connections that cross cultures	a problem		
4	**Analysis and Synthesis** Evaluate Situations Problem Solving **Multiple Perspectives** Debate Brainstorming **Relevance and Significance** Role Playing Simulation	Write to influence, such as to persuade, argue, and request Interpret speakers' messages (both verbal and nonverbal), purposes, and perspectives	Identify the mathematics in everyday situations	Use problem-solving and decision-making skills Understand the importance of individual participation in the democratic process	

Activity	Differentiation Strategies	TEKS: Language Arts and Reading	TEKS: Mathematics	TEKS: Social Studies	TEKS: Science
	Analysis and Synthesis Evaluation Problem Defining Generalizations Trend Extrapolation	Draw conclusions from information gathered from multiple sources	Use addition and subtraction to solve problems involving whole numbers	Understand important issues, events, and individuals of the 19th and 20th centuries.	
		Offer observations, make connections, react, speculate, interpret, and raise questions in response to texts	Use multiplication to solve problems involving whole numbers	Communicate in written, oral, and visual forms	
	Ethics/Unanswered Questions Provocative Questions Problem Sensitivity	Use multiple sources, including electronic texts, experts, and print resources, to locate and organize information.	Use a problem-solving model that incorporates understanding the problem, making a plan, carrying out the plan, and evaluating the solution for reasonableness		
5	**Methodology and Use of Resources** Research Note Taking	Write to inform such as to explain, describe, report, and narrate.			
		Interpret important events and ideas gathered from maps, charts, graphics, video segments, or technology presentations.			
		Summarize and organize ideas gained from multiple sources in useful ways such as outlines, conceptual maps, learning logs, and time lines.			

Activity	Differentiation Strategies	TEKS: Language Arts and Reading	TEKS: Mathematics	TEKS: Social Studies	TEKS: Science
6	**Innovation and Application** Visualization Extend Boundaries **Analysis and Synthesis** Creative Problem Solving Inferences **Multiple Perspectives** Point of View Simulation	Analyze characters, including their traits, motivations, conflicts, points of view, relationships, and changes they undergo Draw inferences such as conclusions or generalizations and support them with text evidence and experience Write to entertain such as to compose humorous poems or short stories			Identify characteristics that allow members within a species to survive and reproduce
7	**Analysis and Synthesis** Analogies Evaluate Situations **Ethics/Unanswered Questions** Tolerance for Ambiguity Provocative Questions **Relevance and Significance** Role Playing Simulation	Offer observations, make connections, react, speculate, interpret, and raise questions in response to texts	Identify the mathematics in everyday situations Use addition and subtraction to solve problems Use place value to read, write, compare and order whole numbers Make generalizations from patterns or sets of examples or nonexamples Select or develop an appropriate problem solving strategy		

77

© **Prufrock Press Inc.**

Activity	Differentiation Strategies	TEKS: Language Arts and Reading	TEKS: Mathematics	TEKS: Social Studies	TEKS: Science
8	**Knowledge and Skills** Categorizing Attributes **Innovation and Application** Visualization Extend Boundaries **Ethics/Unanswered Questions** Provocative Questions Problem Sensitivity	Communicate in written, oral, and visual forms Use problem-solving and decision-making skills			Identify patterns of change such as in weather, metamorphosis, and objects in the sky
9	**Knowledge and Skills** Classifying Research **Multiple Perspective** Debate Brainstorming Inquiry	Frame questions to direct research Write to influence as to persuade, argue, and request		Communicate in written, oral, and visual forms Use problem-solving and decision-making skills Apply critical-thinking skills to organize and use information acquired from a variety of sources Identify different points of view about an issue or topic	
10	**Analysis and Synthesis** Evaluate Situations Critical Thinking Creative Problem Solving **Ethics/Unanswered Questions** Evaluate Situations Problem Defining Provocative Questions		Describe characteristics of data presented in tables and graphs Graph a given set of data using appropriate graphical representation		

78

Activity	Differentiation Strategies	TEKS: Language Arts and Reading	TEKS: Mathematics	TEKS: Social Studies	TEKS: Science
11	**Knowledge and Skills** Attributes Categorizing **Analysis and Synthesis** Provocative Questions Creative Problem Solving **Multiple Perspectives** Point of View Paradoxes	Use his/her own knowledge and experience to comprehend Draw on experiences to bring meanings to words in context such as interpreting figurative language and multiple-meaning words		Offer observations, make connections, react, speculate, interpret, and raise questions in response to texts Write to inform such as to explain, describe, report, and narrate Describe mental images that text descriptions evoke	
12	**Analysis and Synthesis** Evaluate Situations Critical Thinking Analogies **Ethics/Unanswered Questions** Provocative Questions Problem Defining **Communication** Research Demonstration	Adjust reading rate based on purposes for reading. Paraphrase and summarize text to recall, inform, and organize ideas	Identify the mathematics in everyday situations Use addition and subtraction to solve problems Use place value to read, write, compare and order whole numbers Make generalizations from patterns or sets of examples or nonexamples Select or develop an appropriate problem solving strategy		Describe and compare life cycles of plants and animals Compare the adaptive characteristics of species that improve their ability to survive and reproduce in an ecosystem Identify traits that are inherited from parent to offspring in plants and animals

Activity	Differentiation Strategies	TEKS: Language Arts and Reading	TEKS: Mathematics	TEKS: Social Studies	TEKS: Science
13	**Knowledge and Skills** Visualization Demonstration **Innovation and Application** Extend Boundaries Analogical Thinking **Analysis and Synthesis** Draw Conclusions Convergent and Divergent Thinking **Communication** Research Demonstration	Describe mental images and text descriptions evoke Compare oral traditions across regions and cultures Adapt spoken language, such as word choice, diction, and usage to the audience, purpose, and occasion. Interpret and evaluate the various ways visual image makers such as graphic artists, illustrators, and news photographers represent meanings. Generate ideas and plans for writing by using such pre-writing strategies as brainstorming, graphic organizers, notes, and logs. Write to express, discover, record, develop, reflect ideas, and to problem solve.			

80

© Prufrock Press Inc.

Activity	Differentiation Strategies	TEKS: Language Arts and Reading	TEKS: Mathematics	TEKS: Social Studies	TEKS: Science
14	**Multiple Perspectives** Paradoxes Point of View Debate **Ethics/Unanswered Questions** Provocative Questions Tolerance for Ambiguity **Innovation and Application** Analogical Thinking Extend Boundaries	Write to express, discover, record, develop, reflect ideas, and to problem solve.		Use a decision-making process to identify a situation that requires a decision, gather information, identify opinions, and predict consequences	
15	**Knowledge and Skills** Attributes Classifying Categorizing **Methodology and Use or Resources** Inquiry Research **Communication** Writing Skills Uses Technological Media	Determine the purposes for listening such as to gain information, to solve problems, or to enjoy and appreciate Offer observations, make connections, react, speculate, interpret, and raise questions in response to texts Draw conclusions from information gathered from multiple sources	Graph a given set of data using appropriate graphical representation Identify the mathematics in everyday situations		Describe and compare life cycles of plants and animals Compare the adaptive characteristics of species that improve their abilit5y to survive and reproduce in an ecosystem Identify traits that are inherited from parent to offspring in plants and animals.

81

© **Prufrock Press Inc.**

Activity	Differentiation Strategies	TEKS: Language Arts and Reading	TEKS: Mathematics	TEKS: Social Studies	TEKS: Science
16	**Analysis and Synthesis** Aesthetic Thinking Critical Thinking **Multiple Perspectives** Inquiry Point of View **Communication** Decision Making Writing Skills	Read for varied purposes such as to be informed, to be entertained, to appreciate the writer's craft, and to discover models for his/her own writing Determine a text's main (or major) ideas and how those ideas are supported with details Analyze characters, including their traits, motivations, conflicts, points of view, relationships, and changes they undergo Write to entertain such as to compose humorous poems or short stories			
17	**Analysis and Synthesis** Critical Thinking Aesthetic Thinking **Multiple Perspectives** Visual Points of View Visualization **Communication** Art and Geometry Skills Research	Creates mental images from pictures and print Listens to classmates and adults	Knows basic geometric language for describing and naming shapes Understands the characteristics of lines	Organize and interpret information in outlines, reports, databases, and visuals including graphs, charts, timelines, and maps Uses social studies terminology correctly	

82

Activity	Differentiation Strategies	TEKS: Language Arts and Reading	TEKS: Mathematics	TEKS: Social Studies	TEKS: Science
18	**Analysis and Synthesis** Convergent and Divergent Thinking Creative Problem Solving	Offer observations, make connection, reacts, speculate, interpret, and raise questions in response to texts			
	Ethics/Unanswered Questions Provocative Questions Aesthetic Thinking	Interpret important events and ideas gathered from maps, charts, graphics, video segments, or technology presentations			
	Multiple Perspectives Brainstorming Group Consensus				
	Communication Decision Making Writing Skills	Summarize and organize ideas gained from multiple sources in useful ways such as outlines, conceptual maps, learning logs, and time lines			

© Prufrock Press Inc.

Activity	Differentiation Strategies	TEKS: Language Arts and Reading	TEKS: Mathematics	TEKS: Social Studies	TEKS: Science
19	**Knowledge and Skills** Visualization Demonstration **Multiple Perspectives** Brainstorming Point of View **Ethics/Unanswered Questions** Provocative Questions Problem Finding	Write to express, discover, record, develop, reflect ideas, and to problem solvers			

84

Viewpoints

National Standards Checklist

Activity	Language Arts and Reading	Mathematics	Social Studies	Science
1	Uses strategies to write for a variety of purposes			
	Uses as variety of strategies to plan research			
	Uses strategies to gather and record information for research topics			
	Contributes to group discussions			
	Listens to classmates and adults			
2	Uses strategies to write for different audiences	Understands that numbers and the operations performed on them can be used to describe things in the real world and predict what might occur		
	Uses a variety of strategies to plan research			
	Contributes to group discussions			
3	Uses electronic media to gather information	Uses a variety of strategies to understand problem situations		
	Understands the author's purpose			

Activity	Language Arts and Reading	Mathematics	Social Studies	Science
	Makes inferences or Draw Conclusions about characters' qualities and actions			
	Evaluates own and others writing	Understands that data represent specific pieces of information about real-world objects or activities	Civics Knows various people and groups who make, apply, and enforce rules and laws for others and who manage disputes about rules and laws	
	Uses strategies to write for a variety of purposes			
	Uses paragraph form in writing			
4	Uses a variety of strategies to plan research			
	Uses strategies to compile information into written reports or summaries			
	Reads aloud familiar stories, poems, and passages with fluency and expression			
5	Uses prewriting strategies to plan written work	Explain and record observations using objects, words, pictures, numbers, and technology	Geography Knows the similarities and differences in characteristics of culture in different regions	
	Uses a variety of strategies to plan research	Relate informal language to mathematical language and symbols	Understands cultural change	
	Uses strategies to compile information into written reports or summaries		Civics Knows contemporary issues regarding rights	
	Contributes to group			

Activity	Language Arts and Reading	Mathematics	Social Studies	Science
	discussion Uses a variety of strategies to plan research Uses electronic media to gather information Uses prior knowledge and experience to understand and respond to new information		History Knows how to interpret data presented in time lines Understands how people over the last 200 years have continued to struggle to bring to all groups in American society the liberties and equality promised in the basic principles of American democracy History Knows how to interpret data presented in time lines Distinguishes between past, present, and future time	
6	Uses a variety of strategies to plan research Contributes to group discussion	Knows basic geometric language for describing and naming shapes		Knows that living organisms have distinct structures and body systems that serve specific functions in growth, survival, and reproduction Knows different ways in which living things can be grouped and purposes of different grouping
7	Contributes to group discussions Listens to classmates and	Uses trial and error and the process of elimination to solve problems		

Activity	Language Arts and Reading	Mathematics	Social Studies	Science
	adults	Understands the basic difference between odd and even numbers		
		Adds, subtracts, multiplies, and divides whole numbers and decimals		
		Performs basic mental computations		
8	Uses descriptive language that clarifies and enhances ideas			Knows that scientific investigation involve asking and answering questions and comparing answers to what scientist already know about the world
	Uses paragraph form in writing			
	Uses a variety of strategies to plan research			
	Organizes ideas for oral presentations			
9	Uses strategies to write for different audiences			
	Uses a variety of strategies to plan research			
	Uses electronic media to gather information			
	Organizes ideas for oral presentations			

Activity	Language Arts and Reading	Mathematics	Social Studies	Science
	Contributes to group discussion	Understands that data represent specific pieces of information about real-world objects or activities		
	Asks questions in class			
	Responds to questions and comments	Understands that spreading data out on a number line helps to see what the extremes are, where the data points pile up, and where the gaps are		
	Listens to classmates and adults			
10	Organizes ideas for oral presentations	Understands that a summary of data should include where the middle is and how much spread there is around it		
	Listens to and understands persuasive messages			
	Understands techniques used to convey messages in visual media	Organizes and displays data in simple bar graphs, pie charts, and line graphs		
	Understands basic elements of advertising in visual media	Reads and interprets simple bar graphs, pie charts, and line graphs		
		Understands that data come in many different forms and that collecting, organizing, and displaying data can be done in many ways		

Activity	Language Arts and Reading	Mathematics	Social Studies	Science
11	Uses prewriting strategies to plan written work Uses a variety of strategies to plan research Uses strategies to compile information into written reports or summaries Contributes to group discussion	Uses a variety of strategies to understand problem situations Solves real-world problems involving number operations	Geography Knows the similarities and differences in characteristics of culture in different regions Understands cultural change	

Activity	Language Arts and Reading	Mathematics	Social Studies	Science
12	Uses a variety of strategies to plan research Uses electronic media to gather information Contributes to group discussion Organizes ideas for oral presentations Uses a variety of strategies to plan research Uses electronic media to gather information Organizes ideas for oral presentations	Uses explanations of the methods and reasoning behind the problem solution to determine reasonableness of and to verify results with respect to the original problem Adds, subtracts, multiplies, and divides whole numbers and decimals Understands the basic measures perimeter, area, volume, capacity, mass, angle and circumference Organizes and displays data in simple bar graphs, pie charts, and line graphs Knows basic geometric language for describing and naming shapes Performs basic mental computations		Knows that the behavior of individual organisms is influenced by internal cues and external cues, and that humans and other organisms have senses that help them to detect these cues Knows that good scientific explanations are based on evidence (observations) and scientific knowledge Uses appropriate tools and simple equipment to gather scientific data and extend the senses

91

Activity	Language Arts and Reading	Mathematics	Social Studies	Science
	Uses a variety of strategies to plan research			
	Uses electronic media to gather information			
	Creates mental images from pictures and print			
	Understands the ways in which language is used in literary texts			
13	Uses prewriting strategies to plan written work			
	Understands author's purpose			
	Organizes ideas for oral presentations			
	Knows that a variety of people are involved in the creation of media messages and products			
14	Uses prewriting strategies to plan written work			
	Uses a variety of strategies to plan research			
	Organizes ideas for oral presentations			

Activity	Language Arts and Reading	Mathematics	Social Studies	Science
15	Uses prewriting strategies to plan written work Uses a variety of strategies to plan research Organizes ideas for oral presentations	Organizes and displays data in simple bar graphs, pie charts, and line graphs		Knows that plants and animals progress through life cycles of birth, growth and development, reproduction, and death; the details of these cycles are different for different organisms Knows that living organisms have distinct structures and body systems that serve specific functions in growth, survival, and reproduction
16	Writes narrative accounts such as poems and stories Reads aloud familiar stories, poems, and passages with fluency and expression			
17	Creates mental images from pictures and print Listens to classmates and adults	Knows basic geometric language for describing and naming shapes Understands the characteristics of lines	Organize and interpret information in outlines, reports, databases, and visuals including graphs, charts, timelines, and maps Uses social studies terminology correctly	
18	Makes, confirms, and revises simple predictions about what will be found in a text Contributes to group discussion	Uses basic sample spaces to describe and predict events		Knows that scientist and engineers often work in teams to accomplish a task

Activity	Language Arts and Reading	Mathematics	Social Studies	Science
19	Uses strategies to write for a variety of purposes			
	Uses as variety of strategies to plan research			
	Uses strategies to gather and record information for research topics			
	Contributes to group discussions			
	Listens to classmates and adults			

Notes

_____
_____
_____
_____
_____
_____
_____
_____
_____
_____
_____
_____
_____
_____
_____
_____
_____
_____
_____
_____
_____
_____
_____
_____
_____